Why Don't They Cry?

Why Don't They Cry?

UNDERSTANDING YOUR LIVING CHILD'S GRIEF

Zander Sprague LPCC

Copyrighted Material

Why Don't They Cry: Understanding Your Living Child's Grief

Copyright © 2023 by Paradiso Press.

All Rights Reserved.

No part of this publication may be reproduced, stored in a retrieval system or transmitted, in any form or by any means—electronic, mechanical, photocopying, recording or otherwise—without prior written permission from the publisher, except for the inclusion of brief quotations in a review.

For information about this title or to order other books
and/or electronic media, contact the publisher:

Paradiso Press
10 Seminary Ridge Pl
Clayton, CA. 94517
www.paradisopress.com
510-828-8715
publisher@paradisopress.com

ISBNs
Print: 978-0-9795030-4-7 / 0-9795030-4-3
eBook: 978-0-9795030-5-4 / 0-9795030-5-1

Printed in the United States of America

This book is dedicated to Lucy R. Sprague
and all the other siblings who died too soon.

Contents

Dedication	v
Foreword	ix
Acknowledgments	xiii
Chapter 1: The Sibling Survivor Experience	1
Chapter 2: The Sibling Grief	17
Chapter 3: Do Not Be Afraid to Talk to Your Grieving Child	33
Why Communicate?	39
Express Your Feelings	42
Why Do Surviving Children Refuse to Talk It Out?	45
Chapter 4: The "New" Family	49
Source of Inspiration	51
Expectation Varies for Every Child	52
Ask Yourself	54

Story of Jack	60
Let Your Expectations Be Known	64
Chapter 5: The Process of Grief	**67**
Stages of Grief	71
Shock	74
Anger	75
Denial	78
Depression	79
Acceptance	82
Chapter 6: Heal Yourself	**85**
Chapter 7: How Are Your Parents?	**101**
Effects of Negligence	107
High Divorce Rates	109
Forgotten Mourners	114
About the Author	**119**

Foreword

I met Zander when I was a newly minted faculty member. I had graduated with my Ph.D. in Counselor Education and Supervision only a few months prior to our meeting. In that time, I had moved to a new state, been on a job hunt, done many of the things you do when you are acclimating to a new city, and secured a faculty position from said hunt. I was assigned to teach an introductory counseling course in our master's program for my first quarter. I showed up to nearly 50 students in my section, one of whom was Zander.

It was my job to orient both him and his classmates to the counseling profession. Fortunately for both of us, Zander was excited to do the work of learning about the counseling profession. He came to the profession full of empathy for others, a foundational skill in our work, and a clear vision for his future. I also remember Zander jumping into our discussions to ask important questions, push the conversation forward, and share how his experiences shaped his mission and his work with others. Since that class, Zander and I have had the opportunity to work together as colleagues in the counseling profession. He is dedicated to improving the mental health of others. Zander's work has led him to be a licensed professional clinical counselor in California, where he has contributed to our community and is already moving our profession forward into the future.

In all of his endeavors, this book being no exception, Zander invests time, energy, and passion into researching and learning about new topics. This book is a passion project I remember him talking about in some of our first encounters. He has years of experience researching and living with this topic.

I was not familiar with the depth of issues around sibling loss until I met Zander. Thankfully, through his work, I am much more prepared to teach students and help clients learn about grief and sibling loss. I have since learned that nearly 8 percent of the United States' population of adults under the age of 25 will experience the death of a sibling[1]. A sibling loss impacts not only the emotional health of a person, but can also influence their ability to stay in school and their ability to earn an income.[1] Further complicating matters, when someone loses a sibling during childhood, adolescence, or young adulthood, it also impacts their development into adulthood.

This book will be helpful for those who have had the experience of losing a sibling, as well as their friends and mental health professionals who work with them. This book provides the reader a visceral understanding of the intense experience of sibling survivors. As I read this book, I was deeply moved by the stories of others. Zander does an excellent job inviting you into the stories he and others share so you can feel supported or understand the tools needed to support others.

MARGARET LAMAR, PH.D., NCC
Board Certified Counselor
Assistant Professor
Palo Alto University

---

1 Fletcher, J., Mailick, M., Song, J., & Wolfe, B. (2013). A sibling death in the family: common and consequential. Demography, 50(3), 803–826. doi:10.1007/s13524-012-0162-4

Acknowledgments

I would like to acknowledge the Sibling Survivors of The Compassionate Friends, who were so generous with their time in answering my questions. I would also like to acknowledge the many parents to whom I have talked in the last five years, and who inspired this book.

The support of my team and family has been instrumental in making this book happen, and I am forever grateful.

Chapter 1

The Sibling Survivor™ Experience

It's no secret that the longest relationship shared by anyone on Earth is the intimate relationship between siblings. Having a sibling in your life is like having a constant supporter by your side, a "frenemy" who will always motivate you to move forward in your life. They like to build up a competition to help you become more successful than others, even more successful than them. We learn how to communicate and play our roles in society through our siblings.

Siblings play an important role in our life. We either come into this world with a sibling waiting for our arrival, or we step into this world waiting for the arrival of our sibling. It shows how important having a sibling is for a young child. We all expect our siblings to be around us for a very, very long time. It never crosses our mind that we might lose our siblings along the way. We believe that our siblings are going to be there to witness the most important events that will take place in every other stage of our life.

It's natural to assume that your siblings are going to be there to share every joy and tear in your life. It is not so much that we *believe*, it is only because we have been *conditioned* to believe that our siblings are going to be there for us "*forever.*" This is so because we have lived most of our life with them always by our side. Hence, imagine one's shock when they suddenly lose a sibling. Their entire world comes to a halt when they realize that they have lost someone who was a huge part of them. A hole forms in their heart that will forever wait to be filled with someone who has now ceased to exist.

It is worse when someone loses a sibling in the early stages of their life. This does not mean that my loss is any less significant as I grow older and lose a sibling say

The Sibling Survivor Experience

when I am 85 years old who is a couple years younger than me. No, it simply means that, around such an age, both of us would be expecting the other to expire sometime soon. It doesn't lessen the impact of losing someone you love, but it is easier to cope knowing that they died after living out their life. It saves you the trouble of wondering what their life might have been like or how different your life would have been if they hadn't passed away during the earlier stages of their life.

So, what is a sibling survivor? The phrase "sibling survivor" simply points toward those who have lost their sibling and survived through the pain they experienced. Sibling survivors are often called "forgotten mourners" after they lose their sibling(s). Their grief is overshadowed by the grief their parents experience after they lose a child. They become secondary mourners to their own sibling's loss by default.

I work with other sibling survivors to help them cope with their loss and pain. Most of the sibling survivors I work with are between the ages of 18 and 45. That is the time when most of us least expect to lose a sibling in our life. The shock of losing a sibling around such an age can be devastating.

Is it because we spend more of our early years with our siblings as compared to our parents? Dealing with the loss of a young sibling is difficult only because that is the time of our lives that most of us do not necessarily expect to lose a sibling. The loss of a sibling at such a young age first comes with sudden shock. We do not get the time to grieve properly because we are still trying to process what really happened.

Did I really lose my sibling? Are they really dead?

We just can't seem to process the fact that there is a hole in our life that will never be filled, no matter what. Once the news of losing a sibling is completely processed by our minds, we have no other choice but to accept the loss. The people around the sibling survivor make their situation even worse when they come up to them and ask them, *"How are your parents doing?"* Most sibling survivors I have come across and worked with respond that this is the question that bothers them the most after losing a sibling. It is normal for many people to assume what your parents are going through and ask you how they're doing.

The Sibling Survivor Experience

But it can sometimes negatively affect the sibling survivor. It makes them wonder whether the pain they are going through is even worth the acknowledgment. Most sibling survivors have one mindset when no one acknowledges their loss and pain: *How come everyone is asking me about the well-being of my parents and not about mine?* Am *I* not as significant as my parents? Is *my* loss any less than that of my parents? Was the despair *I* was feeling any less than that of my parents? Therefore, your living children are probably being asked how *you* are doing, but they are not being asked how *they* are doing.

This, I believe, has a profound effect on them. It makes them wonder if their loss is somehow not as great as their parents' loss. The first question that came into my mind when people asked how my parents were doing was, *"Is my loss any less significant than my parents'?"* The answer to that question is, of course, "No, not at all; my loss is just as significant." As I said before, the sibling relationship is the longest relationship your child will have in their lifetime, and their sibling, for good or bad, understands them better than they understand themselves.

For many, their brothers and sisters are their confidants. They share every little detail with their siblings. They are the people we go to when we have an issue. As we become adults, we tend to go to our siblings before we go to our parents for a variety of reasons. For one, we simply can never bring ourselves to talk about something serious with our parents for fear of being judged by them or scolded by them. We all know that there is no such thing as "judgment" when it comes to siblings.

Our parents tend to have higher expectations compared to our siblings, and we don't confide in them for fear of letting them down. Some parents who are reading this might be wondering why most siblings confide in each other rather than in me, their parent? There may be a variety of reasons. It may be because siblings do not want to worry their parents about their problems or because they are concerned about their parents' health. Some siblings perceive that their parents treat them as nothing but children for their whole life.

Parents may have more experience in life, but sometimes a child may be too ashamed to present their problems to their parents. The reason why we confide more in our siblings than in our parents is that we trust them enough to help us without letting our parents know. Our siblings are not afraid to break the bitter truth to our face and do not sugarcoat things to lessen the blow.

The sibling survivor experience is unique, and it is different than that of a parent. I am not going to go into detail and talk about what your experience of losing a child is like. As a parent, I don't want to even think about it. I don't know what that is about, and I wouldn't be able to speak about it. Even imagining such a loss sends a shiver of fear down my spine. However, I do know what a loss of a sibling is like. The love shared between siblings is unique, and no one ever seems to understand that until they go through the same loss. We all know that having a sibling is like having a guaranteed best friend by your side. For me, my older sister was one of my best friends. I enjoyed spending my time with her. We went on many trips together. We talked with each other all the time about what was going on in our lives. There was not a detail she was able to miss about my life. Suddenly, after losing her, I had no one to talk to. I had no one to take trips with. I had no one to spend my time with. The shock of her loss hit me intensely, all at once.

We are all aware of the relationship between siblings. We know that it is a very intimate relationship. Most siblings can relate to how they feel for each other. Our siblings tend to be overprotective and sometimes overbearing when they are concerned for us. They don't tend to trust other people in our lives. But, they are also the same people who mess with you just to annoy you. They are always ready to strike down those who bring harm to you, but they don't think twice when they tease you with words that sometimes can turn harsh.

It's okay for them to bully you as long as they are the *only one* bullying you. You know more about your sibling than they know about themselves. You know about every little habit that annoys your sibling, and about *their* habits that seem to annoy *you* as well. If you think about your children when they argue, they tend to swing for the fences. You do not start off nice—you just start arguing and say the meanest

The Sibling Survivor Experience

possible things that you can say to your brother or sister. There is no limit on how much you are willing to hurl mean words at your siblings. That is just the way it is. The reason you are able to do that is because you both have dirt on each other.

You know about their deepest, darkest secrets, and also their silliest secrets that can turn them into the laughingstock of the family. When you fight, you give it your all. But when you love, you give more than what you are capable of offering. That is what it is like to have a sibling by your side. The word "sacrifice" means nothing to you when it comes to giving your sibling what they want. It can be as small as sacrificing a piece of chocolate because it is your sibling's favorite snack, and as big as handing over your concert tickets for your favorite bands because they were unable to get the tickets on time. There are no boundaries when it comes to sharing things with your siblings.

Losing a sibling is not something a sibling survivor can easily "get over." A relationship between siblings is built over the years, and then the shock of it all becomes too much when they suddenly lose their sibling. How can a person even move on if they are not being acknowledged as a mourner? It is that lack of acknowledgment of the loss of our sibling that has a profound effect on us. That effect is something that you, as a parent, are most likely observing but are unable to help your surviving child overcome it.

Now, there is no way to achieve statistically significant proof that losing a sibling has a particular effect on people. I cannot guide every parent out there because I understand that everyone processes grief differently. Everyone has their own coping mechanism when it comes to dealing with pain. But I am going to hypothesize through my work with siblings that there are many siblings out there who turn to alcohol, drugs, or other forms of self-medication in order to get through this loss.

When they feel their loss is not being acknowledged, it only exacerbates that behavior because they believe that no one recognizes the importance of their loss.

"No one seems to recognize what I have lost; I have lost my best friend. I have lost someone who was supposed to be there for me for much longer—my entire life." Now that person is gone, and the rest of the world is not

The Sibling Survivor Experience

acknowledging it. My entire world seems like someone has pressed the "pause" button but is still trying to force the movie to go on.

As a sibling survivor, I can clearly state that it is very challenging, and, again, it has a profound effect on your children when their pain is not acknowledged the way it should be. They feel like no one is talking to them about them. No one is asking how they are. No one is inquiring about what their loss means to them. No one is trying to understand their pain. Again, this is really, really challenging. Through this book, I hope that people are beginning to see some of the challenges that sibling survivors face when it comes to losing their sibling.

I can explain this pain clearly only through an example I came across while working with other sibling survivors. Let us suppose this person named "Jane" has recently lost her brother. She was 25 when her brother suddenly died in a car crash. Like most siblings, Jane was really close to her elder brother, John. He was the family's rock and was the only one who held their family together. His sudden death came as a shock to her. She was not allowed to process

Why Don't They Cry?

her grief, as most of the attention was shifted to her parents and their well-being.

After his death, many people asked how her parents were when she saw them around town. No one bothered to ask how Jane was doing. No one bothered to ask her how she was handling the loss of her brother. As the days turned into weeks and weeks turned into months after her brother's death, Jane was feeling more and more distraught that no one had acknowledged her loss. No one noticed the sudden change in her demeanor. Everyone was focused on helping her parents cope, but no one would help her cope. She was looking for a way to numb that pain. When a person is reduced to a stage where they have to cope with their own pain, they usually choose self-destructive paths.

At first, it started off with having just a glass of wine after work. She would come home every day and drown her loneliness with one glass of wine. Pretty soon, that one glass of wine turned into two, and then two glasses of wine turned into three glasses of wine. But this was not helping Jane at all. It only made her more miserable as time went on. Shortly, she found herself having a glass of wine at lunch. Then on the weekends, she was going out with friends, and she began drinking more than she usually did. In fact, now, she was usually drunk. She spent most of the night crying herself to sleep. And when she would fall asleep, she would always dream about her brother being there in real life.

Waking up to reality day after day in a world where her brother didn't exist left her in a devastating state. She was becoming more and more mentally unstable as time went on. She was feeling that drinking somehow numbed her and made it all better. But clearly, it didn't help her one bit. It was only after a good friend of hers asked how she was doing that Jane began to realize that what she was trying to medicate was a lack of acknowledgment of her pain, which made her question her worth and made her feel like her loss was less than that of her parents. Through some help from a mental professional and an AA program, Jane was able to get her life back together and was finally able to deal with the loss of her brother. It was as if she were seeking others' approval to get some help for herself. Her outlook on life completely changed when she got the help she was secretly seeking after all these months. While others were concerned only about her parents, Jane told herself that she would help herself get through this tough time in her life. Today, Jane is doing much better.

She has taken up exercise to distract herself and is leading a much healthier life. As you can see, there is a lot that happens after the loss of a sibling that goes unacknowledged. This is just one example of how one person was trying to deal with it. It makes me wonder why no one ever bothers to ask a sibling survivor how they are dealing with the loss of their sibling. Whether it is losing an only sibling or losing one out of many siblings, the loss still has a more significant impact on us. Every sibling has a role assigned to them according to their birth order. To suddenly have that order disturbed greatly impacts the other siblings.

Suddenly, a younger offspring is given the responsibilities of the eldest child, or the eldest child becomes the only child. The negative impact begins when people you know are concerned only about your parents.

The Sibling Survivor Experience

Though it makes one grateful to have someone there for your parents, it also makes one wonder, *why is no one there for me?*

As a sibling survivor myself, I can rightfully guide you through the *do*'s and *dont's* when you come face-to-face with a sibling survivor. If you know someone who has lost their sibling recently, do not ask them about how their parents are coping. First, you should ask them about how *they* are dealing with their loss, how it has affected them, and how they are overcoming it.

As painful as it is for a parent to lose a child, it is equally as painful to lose a sibling. The pain of losing someone from your family has different effects on different family members. But nothing compares to the pain a sibling feels when they lose another sibling. When the most important event in your life arrives, you are itching to tell it to a sibling—who no longer exists. These first instincts to inform your sibling about everything in your life is one of the many things that a sibling survivor must learn to suppress. It's heartbreaking to think about it, but the road from there keeps on getting tougher and more challenging for all of the sibling survivors out there.

Chapter 2

The Sibling Grief

S*ometimes death arrives* at our doorstep without any warning. There are two types of death: a death we are expecting (usually linked either to old age or disease with known cause), and the type of death that comes to us in an abrupt manner. Life is not guaranteed, but our mortality is. However, even if humans are aware of the fact that they will have to pass away someday, logic loses all its meaning when someone close to you dies unexpectedly, especially when that someone is a sibling.

When a person is given some sort of warning regarding a loved one's mortality, at least people get a chance to prepare themselves. They get the chance to make amends with them and get to say *"I love you"* one last time. The thing about those who do die abruptly is that they leave us with loose ends. Siblings do fight a lot, and they fight tooth-and-nail when they do. My sister and I also fought from time to time. We always made a ruckus as children.

It is pretty normal for kids to get into useless fights—but they did not seem useless at the time. We would drive our parents mad from time to time like all other young kids do with their parents. All I remember how we would fight one minute, and then our parents would force us to make amends the next. I bet all siblings out there can agree to the fact that fighting between siblings is completely normal and occurs frequently. They get a chance to fight with someone over a completely silly reason and still come out with their sense of justification at the end.

A part of me believes that fighting as kids can only help bring siblings together. Once siblings get immune to the silly fights, which I think is completely possible, they come to rely on each other afterward. It makes me wonder: *Did I fight with my sister because I knew I would be forgiven at the end of the day?* Siblings become each other's safe space. Whenever my sister and I made up after a fight, I got a sense of comfort. We would get closer to each other. A part of me just wishes I had a partner who would forgive me as soon as I apologized.

Sibling love can never be expressed in simple words. We fight a lot, but we also laugh and have fun with each other. We play and goof around all the time whenever we can. As time passes by and we slowly mature into adulthood, obviously we are unable to maintain close contact. We start showing interest in other things. Adulthood changes our schedules, and we start focusing on our own life instead of each other's; that is completely healthy. The sad fact is that not all siblings are able to maintain a healthy relationship as they go on toward the later stages in life.

More often than not, there are fallouts between some siblings that never get resolved during their lifetime. Both parties go on, pretending that the other does not exist. That usually ends up being their biggest regret when one of them passes away unexpectedly. Not everyone shares the same kind of bond with their siblings during their childhood, and it later gets worse as they step into adulthood. Silly fights turn into serious ones, which go beyond repair.

But when you hear the news of someone who passes away and it is someone you fought with the last time you talked, it turns out to be one of your greatest regrets. Even if the fights were quite severe, it all seems miniscule once the person passes away. It becomes meaningless when the person you are fighting with, your own sibling, ceases to exist. People regret it when they are unable to say they were sorry. They are not able to tie up those loose ends when someone dies out of the blue, and this can greatly affect someone quite negatively.

For all you know, the last thing you told your sibling before they passed away was how much you hate them, even if it was done humorously. Maybe the last thing you said might have hurt your sibling. The possibilities of everything ending horribly are endless. You think you have all the time in the world to make up, but that thinking changes when you lose someone unexpectedly. Then you don't get the chance to take it back because they are no longer going to be there for you.

One of the most important rules in life is to remember that once you say something or do something, you might never get the chance to take it back. You might never get the chance to see them again. You might never get the opportunity to make amends, and that can go on to haunt you later in life. Every life near you is precious, so treat that life with high importance before it is snatched away from your grasp.

They say that grief comes in the same form to everyone. That's not true. Grief comes in many forms, and it comes with different intensities. Losing a sibling is not easy, and it is even harder when your sibling passes away in unforeseen circumstances. You wake up one day and finally realize that they are really gone, and then it hits you.

The grief hits you in tidal waves as the numbness wears off and leaves you in a confused pile of mess. *How?* That is the only question in your mind as you try to process what you are feeling. The worst realization of all is knowing that you cannot take back what you said to them last, whether or not it was a joke. You are deprived of *closure*. You start craving it with every breath you take, and that can have a long-lasting effect on anyone, like a deep scar. Regret is always there, rooted deep into your heart as you try to admit the fact that your loved one, with whom you had a falling-out, is now gone. Or a sibling who passed away before you could tell them how much they meant to you or how much you loved them. Life snatches away the opportunity from you, and you start blaming the world around you. When you get tired of blaming the world, you start to blame yourself. *"If only I had not said that." "If only I could tell them how much I loved them for one last time." "If only I could hug them again."* Your life is dictated by all such *ifs* going on in your mind, and you are forever stuck wondering what it would have been like if only you had *known*.

The thing about sibling grief is that, no matter how much you are breaking on the inside, you try never to show it to your parents on the outside. As a parent myself, I would do anything for my daughters if they came to me for something. I believe that it is my duty to look after my kids before I look after myself. This protective feeling a parent has is completely natural.

The Sibling Grief

It is an inborn trait that is activated when you finally hold your newborn in your arms for the very first time.

You can surely develop such feelings over the years, but everything that grows has roots to grow from. These roots are planted into us from the moment of our birth. We all come into this world believing we have a purpose of our own. Some believe their purpose is to protect someone until they are old enough—and strong enough—to do it themselves. One of the many things that psychologists around the world have failed to do is completely learn human nature. Every human has a different nature, and hence; they cannot be boxed into one category.

However, despite knowing that your parents are going to be there for you, a sibling survivor refuses to go to them in the middle of their mental breakdown. They believe they have to be strong for their parents. They have to be resilient. Such feelings lead only to them feeling complicated with their own feelings. They are stuck between wanting to comfort and wanting to be comforted. Such contradictory feelings can lead the sibling survivors to feeling utterly useless.

I remember the time when my sister was murdered. I remember how silent the chaos had been in my parents' heads. Even at the age of twenty-eight, all I wanted to do was go to my parents and cry to them. I wanted to wrap my arms around my parents and tell them anything that would take their pain away, even when I knew that nothing I could say would ease or lessen their suffering. I also wanted them to say something that could ease the ache in my heart.

It was a confusing moment—I wanted to take care of them, *and* I wanted them to take care of me. I could not bring myself to go to them and say, *"It's hard for me. Hold me, please. Take care of me now."* I could not say that. I wanted to say that, but I did not want to add to their burdens. I could clearly see how much grief my mother was in, how much she was hurting, and I was not about to add to her burden with my sorrows.

The age group of the sibling survivors I am working with can relate to the level of uneasiness that I felt in front of my parents after my sibling's death. They felt like joining the crying fest with their parents, but they did not want to shatter their souls by making them see how much the surviving sibling was hurting as well. The sibling survivor thinks that it is not the right time to go to their parents. And later on, some think that it is too late to talk about their pain. The case gets severe with adults who refuse to go to their parents regarding their pain. The adult sibling survivors always confess how they do not want to seem childish by troubling their parents with their sorrow. It is a perception that life teaches adults to deal with themselves, for better or for worse.

This world constantly teaches children how they should act when they ascend from childhood into adolescence and, finally, into their adulthood. Adulthood is like that Stop signal that says, *"Don't go any further"* when it comes to talking to your parents regarding certain issues. Most adults are made to feel by societal values like they are old enough to deal with anything themselves, and so they refuse to go to their parents for solace.

They believe that their pain is no longer supposed to be their parents', as the parents have suffered enough. For better or worse, they believe that it is time for them to deal with their own grief. The thing about grief is that it never leaves you if you suffer through it alone. Because you refuse to open up to others, grief is always at the back of your mind, constantly reminding you of what has happened. Talking to a psychologist might help someone, but talking to a relative who can relate to your level of pain can alleviate your grief.

Despite having a great relationship with my parents, it got harder for me to talk about my sister as I grew up. We used to talk about my sister's death a lot in the first few years after she was murdered, but it got more challenging as time went on. So much time had passed that I rarely cried in front of my parents again regarding her death. It was not like I didn't feel the pain as time went on.

It was just the fact that I knew I was old enough to deal with it myself. I learned how to bury the grief because I thought my pain was insignificant compared to my parents'. I did not want to remind them again and again about the grief that was still fresh in their minds. Losing a loved one, especially someone who is your child, leaves a scar that might never heal. For a sibling survivor, it becomes a scab that they refuse to *let* heal. In order to remind themselves, they peel off that scab but refuse to cry about it. I didn't want them to become aware of the gaping hole in my life. Other siblings have said the same thing when I bring this up in my workshops.

"Why don't you cry in front of your parents?" I would ask them after telling them about my own experiences. They would agree that they did not want to add to their parents' hurt by further talking about someone who is just not there anymore. Sibling survivors, more often than not, forget about their pain and focus more on that of their parents, who are suffering in ways that the surviving siblings cannot understand. The adults know that the parents are just trying to get by themselves, with their own pain; the sibling survivors avoid adding to their burdens.

Sometimes our parents need some space and time before they can resume taking care of their children. As adults, they understand that their parents are also only human beings who are trying to process their own grief. It does not make the process any easier for either party, but it helps the parents to understand that their children are trying to deal with the pain in a similar manner. Children are good at mimicking. They imitate their parents in order to look mature. Everyone is trying to find their own way through this situation, constantly looking for different ways to deal with this grief. They need to gain perspective in their lives to continue to live on.

While researching for this book, I wanted to do my best to convey both sides of the stories. I wanted to speak from the main perspective of the sibling, but I also wanted to put some of my focus on the parents, who had it tough as well. I came across some parents who were going through this tough time where they had to deal with their surviving child and asked them a few questions regarding it.

"Have you seen your living child grieve in front of you?" I asked them. Almost every one of them said that they were aware of the fact that their living children were grieving. They just never saw them grieve in front of them. Their children would hide their pain behind a calm mask because, in their minds, they had to be stronger for the parents, who, unintentionally, would break down in front of them from time to time.

The Sibling Grief

One of the stories I came across was a woman named Carol. Her story was absolutely devastating. She had lost one of her sons in the military. She had been looking for ways to help her living child. Carol always expressed how her son used to come to her for many things before but now, he hardly showed up. Every time she tried to talk to him, he would always say, *"Mom, I'm fine. I'm dealing with this."* His mother's intuition, however, told her otherwise. She knew he was not okay and she knew her son was merely trying to hide his struggles. Carol just could not figure out how to make her son talk. She wanted him to open up to her instead of keeping it all to himself. She wanted to ask why he was not coming to her as he always had. Carol expressed her deep concern regarding the matter of her son shutting himself up in his room.

Carol's son attended one of my workshops, and I asked him why he was not opening up to his mother anymore. He broke down in front of me and said, *"I was not about to add to what was already a huge burden on her life."* He opened up and told me how he would hold himself back because he knew how distraught she was on a daily basis. He noticed how his mother would cry every time she passed by his brother's picture. *"It breaks my heart to see her like that,"* he said.

A part of me understood why he was saying that. As a child myself, I don't want to see my parents in pain. My daughters seem instinctively to notice my sudden shift in mood, which is further evidence for me that we are born like that. All Carol's son wanted was a hug from his mom, and cry to her, but the feeling that he was being a "burden" always held him back from going to his mother to talk about his grief.

After listening to him, I encouraged and advised him to share his feelings with his mother openly. He might not want to add to her burden, but having her worry about him while going through her own grief was going to adversely affect her even more. I told him that his mother was concerned about him as well and that the best thing he could do was talk to her. It would give her a gateway to talk to someone who could understand her level of pain.

I helped facilitate the beginning of that conversation. They were quite surprised to understand what was lurking inside their minds. Their grief was different from each other's, but it hurt them all the same. Both of them had lost someone important in their lives, and both were facing the same trial, one that they presumed was different for each. Little did they know that the pain would only help them grow closer together. To make sure that they understood each other, I gave them advice that helped them change their lives.

Chapter 3

Do Not Be Afraid to Talk to Your Grieving Child

One of my main pieces of advice to all the parents out there is to reach out to your children *despite* the circumstances holding you back. Do not be afraid to talk to your grieving child. A lot of fears might be holding you back from taking the initiative. You do not know whether your child is ready for "the talk"—and, no, I'm not talking about the one you have when they reach puberty.

This talk is far more sensitive and so painful that it makes you wonder if you will get through it without breaking down yourself. This talk is about how they are now one of the "sibling survivors," and what their position in the family is. As stated previously, the birth order has now changed after the loss of their sibling. Before, you just assumed that your child understood their new position, but now, it is vital for you to talk to them to help them understand their new position.

Most survivors who come to me during my workshops do not even know what their status becomes after losing their sibling. "Sibling Survivor" is a difficult identity to embrace because no one is ready to openly talk about it. Either most refuse to label themselves as such because it makes them feel guilty or those who accept it, feel like they are victimizing themselves. Your grieving child may seem like a ticking bomb to you, but the truth is, they are just being cautious in order not to hurt you. As a parent, you know your children better than anyone else. You know when your surviving child is pushing you away.

The reasons for that may vary, but parents who rely only on assumptions and try to "make it better" simply compound the harm. The child knows that their parents are only trying to help them, but *their* main focus is making sure their parents feel that they

Do Not Be Afraid to Talk to Your Grieving Child

don't have to pay any attention to *them*. Don't push your child farther away by acting on your assumptions alone. Your children are slowly pushing themselves out of your life, and you cannot afford to lose another child who is right in front of you.

As a parent myself, I can understand how scary it can be for you to see your living child in such a state. I know how a parent cannot stand to see their children cry.

My daughters manage to make me feel bad when they are crying for a mere toy at a store, so I cannot imagine what the grieving parents must be going through to see their living children cry. Parents need guidance to understand that they do not need to jump to conclusions and start thinking about what would "make it better" for them. Most parents tell me how they are trying to do things to cheer them up like cooking their favorite dinners or even making their favorite dessert.

Some parents buy their living child material things or sign them up for therapy sessions. But this will most probably backfire, because their main goal is to make sure you are not focusing on them. No amount of therapy sessions or favorite dinners is going to make them forget about one of the biggest losses in their lives. I do think that therapy can be, and is, very helpful, but connecting with your child is the most important.

They are too young to go through such pain, and they don't know how to deal with it. As a parent, you need to be one-on-one with your children. No one can replace the child you lost, but you can still make sure that your living child does not push you out of their life. Make sure you talk to your living children and tell them to open up. Tell them how much it hurts you to see them pull themselves away from you. Tell them how concerned you are by their behavior.

Tell your living child that it only adds to your pain seeing them pull away from you. Trust me—your child will not hesitate to open up to you the moment you tell them that it is *okay* for them to do so. They need a little confirmation with the fact that *their* grievances matter, too, and that it is okay for them to talk to their parents about it.

The psychology of the living children gets a little complicated. After they lose someone as close to them as a sibling, they do not understand where they stand in the family. They lose the sense and security of their position and are no longer comfortable with their circumstances. During these times, when the living child is completely at a loss for what to do, all they need is some sort of sign, a validation to tell them that it is *okay* for them to come to you. They are holding themselves back only for the sake of their parents. You, the parent, already know the psychology of your children like the back of your hand. But, at this given moment, you are in the middle of all this chaos and confusion that makes you lose all confidence in yourself. It is normal for a parent's confidence to waiver from time to time. All of us question whether what we are doing, the steps we are taking is best for our children. They become our prime focus, and, naturally, we feel responsible for bringing another human into this world. For most, a child is like a ray of hope.

They take it as an opportunity for redemption and do their best to provide the comforts of this world to their children. I believe that a person loses the sense of "me" and reaches the sense of "we" after the birth of their child. This means that they are no longer single players but team players. In a sense, it also helps in bringing the spouses closer together, as they finally have something that can knot them closer together—their child. A parent's confidence shatters when they lose their child. Shattering of confidence leads only to further complications in their life.

Parents are always quick to blame themselves when something happens to their children. Sure, children make their own choices in this life—some of which can potentially lead to their demise. But for a parent, there is this guilt in the back of their minds that *if only* they had raised their kids better or looked after them better, they could have saved them. The sorrow intensifies when such thoughts totally consume them until all they are left with is a lifeless corpse.

It gets worse when the parents feel as if they no longer know the person their living child is slowly evolving into. They are evolving in order to protect you from their grief, and, in that way, the living child loses the sense of their suffering. They hold themselves back in fear of triggering their parents in a way that leaves them a crying mess in your bedroom. A child sees their parents as their rock—those special people who help them feel grounded.

Seeing you grieve and break down makes them realize that their hero-like parents are mere mortal human beings, just like them. They realize that their parents have the right to grieve and have their own space. After all, the living child believes that it is time to become the rock of their family in their parents' stead. In order to avoid conflict for both parties, it is essential for them to open up to each other. I will not lie and say it is going to be easy. It is going to be painful in ways you have never experienced before. The emotions you feel will be so raw and deep that they will leave you an emotional mess.

So, why is it that I am advising most people to talk to their living child if it is so painful? I guess that can further be explained as we move on with this chapter. After all, a person should become patient enough to take one step at a time.

Why Communicate?

Communication makes this world an easy place. Can you imagine what the world would be like if people simply refused to communicate with each other? In order to make yours and your child's life easier, communication is vital. Do not be afraid to talk to your grieving child about your pain. Show them that it is okay for them to express their feelings to you. It is easier said than done when I tell people to talk to their grieving child. They think it is absurd of me to say it to their face: *"Talk it out."*

I would always advise the parents and children alike. Everyone who comes to my workshop knows what I have been through. The first thing I tell them is my own story, so that they can develop a sense of familiarity. No one can come to me and say, *"Easy for you to say. You don't know what we're going through!"* They know exactly what I am going through, and I know exactly what they're going through.

Over the years, I have talked about my story. I tell them how my sister was killed and what kind of impact it had on me. They would all listen closely to my story. Most of the sibling survivors come to me and ask how I can talk about my sister without having a complete mental breakdown, because, for them, it is utterly impossible to do so. Their loss is still fresh in their minds. *"Does it get better with time?"* Some have asked.

No, time does not heal us completely. Time merely tells us how to deal with it. We get used to the pain over the years, to the point that it simply stops aching. But just because there is no aching pain, it doesn't mean that it's not hurting us. Even now, it hurts me deeply when I think about how different my life would be if my sister were alive today. My daughters would have someone they could call "Aunt." The possibilities of what it would be like are endless, and thinking about it still evokes deep emotions within me. I just learned how to stop that deep ache from hurting, with the passage of time. I do not believe that I have been desensitized to the grief—I believe that I have merely learned how to process through it.

The loss I suffered pushed me to help others who are going through the same pain. Even though the help that I provide to those suffering through the same trauma I have been through may seem minimal, it still has a great impact on people. Talking about my sister from time to time helped me understand my own feelings. In a way, it feels as if talking about her will somehow keep my memories of her alive.

Express Your Feelings

Feelings can be extremely fragile around such a sensitive period in your life. A parent believes that nothing can compare to the pain they feel when they lose a child. They remember the joy they felt after the birth of their children. Life seemed a little brighter and the experiences were more joyful. You get to see your child grow right in front of you. You get to observe every little detail; you pick up their habits, and they pick up yours. It feels as if someone has snatched away all of your joy when the child dies. To see your child die painfully becomes an even more traumatizing experience for you. It feels like the end of the world as you knew it. Nothing makes sense to you anymore. A strange sense of numbness falls over your mind. When that numbness leaves, you finally grasp the severity of your situation.

No one can imagine what it feels like to have your child with you one minute and then snatched away from you the next? It is easy as a parent to be so wrapped up in your own grief that you forget you are not alone in this loss. Your surviving children feel the same level of pain that you do. For them, someone has snatched away their play buddy, their go-to person, and their safety blanket.

Most siblings hold each other dear and close to their hearts. I have seen older siblings express their grief over the loss of their younger sibling. Many feel as if they have failed—as the elder one—to keep their younger sibling safe. They regret how they always pushed their younger sibling away whenever they sought out their attention. I mean, it is something all elder siblings do. *"I'm too busy—maybe later."* Realizing that the "later" never came, they feel as if they have failed as a sibling. And, I have seen younger siblings look lost when they express their grief over the fact that they have lost someone who was as close to them as a guardian angel. They feel as if they did not protect them the way they should have protected them. Their feelings are hardened, like glass that can easily be shattered if it is not taken care of properly.

Why Don't They Cry?

Both elder and younger siblings may be standing on different sides, but they regret it all the same. As a parent, there should be no shame when it comes to expressing your feelings to your children. Most parents believe that they have to hide their vulnerable side from their children in order to appear strong.

You do not want your child to see you shatter, similar to the way your child does not want you to see them shatter. It is imperative to end that thinking process and to come together and help each other out with your respective grief. Quit holding yourself back from expressing your feelings to your children. Tell them that you know it hurts and that it is tough for them. Talk to them, and assure them that you can get through this together.

"I don't have to process this grief alone, kid. I know it's tough for you, and seeing you hide your pain is even tougher on me. It's okay to cry in front of me; it's okay to burden me. I am your parent; nothing burdens me more than not knowing what is going on inside you. It's okay to tell me when your hurting. I'm your parent. I am here for you."

Show them your vulnerable side. It is okay for them to see that side of you every once in a while. This reminds them that their parents, too, are only human beings just trying to get by in this world.

Why Do Surviving Children Refuse to Talk It Out?

Most surviving children refuse to open up in order not to burden you with their problems. They will not understand that your burden only increases when they hold themselves back from you. Guide your children regarding this matter, and tell them they should stop holding themselves back. Remember that they are your children, no matter how old they are, and that they will always seek your approval and guidance when it comes to such sensitive matters. When your child is an adult and becomes a parent himself/herself, explain it to them by asking them to stand in your shoes. Ask them, *"What would you rather have your child do in such a situation? Would you rather have them hold back or come to you?"* Both parties, the parent and the surviving child, have lost so much in a day. Nothing can compensate for all of your pain, but talking about it with someone who gets it makes it a little more bearable. Having someone there for you can ease your ache a little bit. The ache goes away, step by step, as you sit down together with your living child to pour out your feelings.

Most living children miss out on the opportunity of telling their parents how they really feel. You cannot push your child into talking to you. Go to them every day, and subtly tell them that you, the parent, are always available whenever they need it. But, make sure you are as accessible to your child as you assure them you are. Express your gratitude when they do open up, because it's tough for them—they feel like they are further burdening you. Life is full of surprises, some of which hit you harder than others. However, these surprises need to be figured out together with your loved ones.

You will want to express your feelings to your children, and assure them that it is okay for them to break down in front of you. No matter what, your relationship cannot go back to the way it was before the loss occurred. The sense of loss may never leave you. The main point is to make your child feel comfortable opening up to you. It is okay for them to cry in front of you because their loss is just as significant as yours. At the same time, you will need to express your feelings to your children; tell them that you are all in this together and together, you will get through this. Tell them that you are now a team, going through one of the most unbearable losses. Talk to them about death. Tell them how death is a part of our life.

We come into this world with the tag of death attached to our souls. Explain it to them in a way that they can use to process through losses when you are no longer there. A parent needs to prepare their child for the future, in case the inevitable occurs. What better way is there than talking about it? It will take a lot of time for your grieving child to open up. They might not even talk the first time you mention it. They might cry, throw tantrums (depending on child's age), and tell you that you are wasting your time. They will do their best to divert the attention away from themselves.

Be prepared to deal with their reaction and be patient through it. They might even anger you to the point that you might burst. But remember, these children are holding themselves back for your sake only. They want you to have some space. You become one of their main priorities because they feel like you have no one to rely on. As a parent, remind them that they are your children and should be acting as such.

Most surviving siblings face some sort of identity crisis as they wonder where they stand in their family now. It feels as if their positions have been forsaken due to the loss of their sibling. Gently guide them, and tell them that, no matter where they stand, they are still your child and will be loved by you all the same. A family that loses a child can never be the same way it used to be.

Not only are they forced to live as "A New Family"—they are also forced to burden their children with a new position within the family order. If a child is made to feel as if they are their sibling's replacement, it just gets more difficult to cope with their pain from that point forward. As a parent, you will want to make sure your child feels safe enough with their grief to talk about it.

Chapter 4

The "New" Family

We all come into this world with a specific order. This order is known as the *"birth order,"* and it decides what kind of vital role we will be playing in our family. The thing about birth order is that it is not assigned to us by someone else. We are inevitably born with these orders that are handed to us by nature. Psychology says that parents are more excited about their first baby than they are about their second one. That does not mean that parents love their first child more than their second or any other children that are born to parents. It merely says that humans are always excited about their "first times."

Why Don't They Cry?

When the first baby is born, parents go through the process of preparing themselves mentally, so that they can get into the mindset of "parents." When the first child arrives, there are a lot of "first times" for you as parents. Mothers get to experience the baby's kick in the womb for the first time. You get to see the baby crawl for the first time. You get to look at the baby walk for the first time and progress little by little. All humans tend to be excited when they make up their minds to try out new things in life. This also means that the new parents focus more on learning many things through their first newborn. This first child becomes the subject of all sorts of experimentation for parents. You get to slowly learn about parenting, step by step, since parenting is an endless learning process.

Many eldest siblings assert that their parents were stricter with them as compared to their younger siblings. They may complain that their parents allow their younger siblings to do things the elder sibling was not allowed to do. Many parents confess to being stricter with their eldest child since they believe that their eldest child should be capable of setting a certain standard for their younger siblings.

Source of Inspiration

It's a fact that many younger siblings look up to their elder siblings. They like to act out the same way their elder sibling would act out. Many parents even taunt their children during small moments of anger and say, *"Don't be impressed by your elder sibling!"* As a parent myself, I noticed how my youngest child likes to copy my eldest child. As someone who grew up with an elder sibling, I always wanted to follow my sister around when we were kids. No matter how much we fought, I still sought her approval. As I said, the bond shared between siblings is sacred and cannot be described with mere words.

However, we can all agree that it is a natural cycle, followed by everyone in the world. We all want to have someone to look up to. We want someone who can become a source of inspiration, someone who can guide us without having any hidden agendas. That someone, most of the time, happens to be our eldest sibling.

Hence, the birth order plays an essential role in assigning us our duties. This natural cycle of raising the first child in a stricter environment is because many parents have different expectations of their various children. A first child is most likely to be more responsible and mature as compared to the second or third child. This is only because of the expectations they grew up with. The eldest child is raised with the mindset of taking care of their younger siblings.

Have you not noticed how childish the youngest child of any household can be? They are usually labeled "the pampered royalty" by most of their elder siblings. The youngest child is more likely to be immature and impulsive since they are the "baby" of the house and are doted on by everyone in the family from time to time. Age does not matter for siblings—the youngest can be thirty-five and still be treated like a pampered child by their siblings or their parents.

Expectation Varies for Every Child

This powerful bond is not entirely broken but somehow shaken up as one of the siblings passes away. The

The "New" Family

birth order waivers, and the parents no longer know how to shift the responsibilities from one sibling to another. In my case, my eldest sister was the rock of the family. I believe she was raised with all of the responsibilities drilled into her head.

There were a lot of expectations that were placed on her. After she passed away, those expectations fell on me. Suddenly, I had to become the trailblazer for my family. I became the person to do everything for the first time in my family. My sister passed away when she was thirty years old.

After her death, I became the first child to reach the age of thirty-one, thirty-five, and forty, and so on. I became the first one to do many things that are considered to be milestones in someone else's life. Out of nowhere, the duties of the eldest child fell on my shoulders, and I had no idea how to deal with the new order given to me.

Birth orders are rearranged after a child in the family passes away. If the eldest child dies, the second or middle child becomes the eldest one. Or if the youngest one dies, the second-youngest child becomes the youngest. These changes are not easy to deal with. In some cases—when parents have only two children and the eldest sibling dies—the second child becomes the only child.

This transition of birth order shakes up everyone in the household. This reordering of siblings affects the entire family. These effects are not restricted to the sibling survivors; the parents are also affected. Each parent has a set of expectations placed on each one of their children, and suddenly, these expectations need to be placed on someone else's shoulders. Siblings understand this and do their best to cope with the change.

The only way to cope with this is by coming together and talking to each other about it. After all, the "New Family" needs to come together to understand what kind of roles they have to play later in life.

Ask Yourself

The parents need to ask themselves what their reaction toward their living children is like? What kind of expectations do you have for your living child that you never had before? Have you talked to them about the expectations you hold for them?

The "New" Family

Many parents become quite possessive of their children after losing one of their children. They have this fear of "failing to protect" the living children and go to any lengths to keep them safe. It is okay to understand that there are things that scare you now—things that may seem mundane to every other person out there.

There comes a point where as a parent, you want to do nothing but keep your living child close to you. You would go to any lengths to make sure that your living child is safe. You lose all rationality when it comes to keeping your living child safe. Grieving parents know that they cannot keep their children safe forever, but their terror stops them from listening to that rational voice. I remember how protective and defensive my parents were after they lost my sister. At one point, my father even confessed that all he wanted to do was to lock me and my younger sister up in the house so that nothing dangerous could happen to either of us.

He knew that he could not act on his impulsive emotions, but he still worried about us more than he had before. It took a lot for him to confess something so heartbreaking to us, and his efforts were appreciated. I knew he was saying that only because he wanted to keep us safe and was afraid of losing yet another child. It was an entirely understandable reaction that every parent must go through. He would have kept us locked up in the house if it was possible, but he realized that no amount of locking us up could keep us safe or sane.

His words to me, to this very day, mean so much.

"I want to make sure you're safe, and the best way to keep you safe is for you to not be out in the world, where someone can hurt you." He also said, *"But I know I can't do that."*

After working with other sibling survivors and sometimes with the "new family," it is common for parents to want to know where their children were at all times. They started keeping tabs on their children by asking their living children to check in with them whenever they reached their destination safely.

"Call me when you get home."
"Call me when you reach the market."
"Check in with me when you get to the mall."

The "New" Family

As a parent who has suffered losing a child you become afraid of sending your surviving children out into the world fearing they might be snatched away too. As an adult, we can understand the parent's intentions and that they are not misplaced. However, this sudden change is severe and so swift that your living child might need a year or two to understand their role.

The new expectations manifest themselves in many different ways. Your living child might be doing their best to meet your expectations because they want to do nothing more than make you happy. They carry the burden that comes with carrying new expectations for your sake.

Your child might react and rebel against this by saying something like, *"No, you don't get to have that access into my life because you never tried before, and you are not getting it now."* As parents, do your best to understand where your grieving child is coming from. Most sibling survivors might see these expectations as suffocation. Many times, members of the "new family" want to begin vacationing together to emphasize how important the living children are to them and to connect with them differently. These family vacations can be enjoyable and sometimes end with positive results. However, it might not be something your living child wants or is ready for so soon after their loss. The living children might not come forward and tell the parents about how they feel about everything.

This is where communication plays an essential role. To understand the intentions of both sides, this new family needs to realize that keeping feelings suppressed is not going to help their case in any way. Avoiding communication may make things worse as everyone tries to tiptoe around each other instead of sitting down and talking it out. Communication helps the family maintain the balance they need to get on with their life. Communicate with them—not as children but as adults, peer to peer.

You may ask them, *"What are you doing?"*

"Can you explain to me why you are making that choice?"

Tell them that you are not trying to be nosy or intrusive but that you are trying to understand them on a specific level. If you get curious, don't ask them

The "New" Family

questions to the point that they turn defensive. Ask them the right questions subtly. Instead of asking them why they are displaying a specific behavior, let it play out before calming your child down.

The kids will not understand what is going through your mind, so you need to tell them that you do not understand them. Share your feelings with them the same way my father shared something profound with my sister and me. This helped me understand the mindset of my parents and how mentally damaged my father was over the death of my sister.

All he wanted to do was keep us all safe, even at the cost of being hated by us. I could understand him better after he shared his feelings with us. It was helpful in explaining where he was coming from, and it allowed me to understand the decisions he would come to make later in our lives. There were a lot of times he would get upset by my choices.

A lot of changes happened after my sister passed away. At the time, I was living in Boston, and I decided to move to California shortly after her death. My father was very upset about this, and it scared him. I understood his reaction once he had disclosed his feelings to me. It made everything so much easier, and I was able to interact with him because I realized what his perspective was based on.

Story of Jack

One of the unique cases I came to face-to-face with after opening a workshop for other sibling survivors was that of Jack. Jack was a middle child of three. He was twenty-two years old when his older sister passed away. With Jack's family background, the oldest child was trained to take on many responsibilities. The oldest child was expected to do many things. It was a part of the cultural history of Jack's family.

The oldest child was talked to on a daily basis to help them understand their roles. Stories were told, and examples were drilled into their minds which helped them understand what their position was going to be as the oldest child. Now, all of a sudden, at the age of twenty-two, Jack had to learn all of these things from scratch. He had spent most of his life oblivious to certain things. After his sister's death, his parents turned to him and said, *"You're the*

The "New" Family

oldest now, and you need to be doing these things from now on." The transition was shocking for Jack, and he even told me how challenging it was for him to accept this. It was culturally expected of Jack, now being the oldest, there were many responsibilities he didn't previously have.

Now, Jack would be expected to be there to take care of his parents as they age. It was now his responsibility to be the one who would show his younger brother how to go out and do things in the world. Jack told me that this was a tough transition for him, especially in the first five years because he did not have any expectations of the role of the eldest sibling before, and now, he was not familiar with these duties. He had not been what we would call *"trained."* He was raised differently than his elder sibling had been and now suddenly, his parents were placing all of these responsibilities on him.

Jack felt as if his parents were not very understanding. They just assumed that he knew what to do. Jack was finally able to find his voice and say, *"I understand and accept the responsibilities that I now have. However, I need some help because I haven't had any training in how to do this. I sort of know, but I'm not sure."* So, he sat down with his parents, and they talked about what these expectations were. Jack pushed back on some of it. There were some things he was not able to accept, and some of that, I think, was due to the cultural difference. His parents were first-generation immigrants who had grown up with a belief system that they brought from the country they immigrated from into the United States. Jack had grown up in the United States, where there are perhaps fewer expectations as compared to his parents' people back at home.

Jack told me that it had been ten years since his sister died and that he sort of negotiated with his parents about what he was willing to do and what he wasn't. He explained how his perspective was different from theirs. Jack said that there had been some tension from time to time and that there still was some, but he was able to find a way to talk to his parents about it.

Communication made it easier for him to cope with the changes and responsibilities. As a parent, it is imperative for you to tell your living children what your expectations are for them. It is an undeniable fact that

The "New" Family

your expectations for the living children change after the loss of one child. You need to discuss the responsibilities with them and discover what they are willing to take on and what they aren't. Their opinion on this change matters as much as your opinion does. You need to have an open mind and keep this discussion going with them. You are not going to have a list of expectations ready for them immediately, but it is important to pay close attention to them. Do not get frustrated when your living child doesn't fulfill your expectations because, half of the time, they don't know that they need to do something that you think they should be doing.

As a parent, you need to think twice before placing a particular set of expectations on them. You need to ask yourself whether the expectations you are putting on your living children are fair or not. Are you sure you are asking them to do something they are capable of? You cannot simply expect them to understand the "new" role they are supposed to take on after the death of their sibling nor do it as well as them.

The gap left by the sibling is far too vast for that, and no amount of hard work is going to fill it up. Your living child might do everything in their power to fill the gap, but to a certain limit, it is never going to be enough for either of you. Talking about these expectations rather than just sitting back and assuming they will be fulfilled is a foolish play on the part of the parent.

Let Your Expectations Be Known

Expectations are something that everyone has. It is inevitable for you not to expect anything out of someone. After all, it is a human emotion that cannot be denied by anyone in this world. But it will be frustrating and fruitless if your living child does not have a clue that you are expecting them to play a certain role. In order for your living child to understand their new role better, you need to tell them what the expectations are for them. You, as a parent, might lose the opportunity to make sure that your child fulfills your expectations if you do not communicate verbally and openly.

Arguments take place in many families because one person has a certain expectation of another that is not being met. More frustration and turmoil arise between the members of this "New Family" instead

The "New" Family

of understanding and love. As a sibling survivor, I would like to encourage every parent to pay close attention to what they are expecting from their living child in the new family.

You need to think about whether it is fair to place these expectations upon your living child. The disruption of the natural birth order leaves the sibling survivors with a deep wound that can never be healed. The absence of that dead sibling resonates loudly in this "New Family" because everyone is clueless and does not know what kind of roles they have to play now—the sibling order is now reshuffled. After the loss of a child, you are left with a family who has no idea how to behave around each other.

No one has any idea how to act around their family members. At some point, your living children might even feel like they can't fit into their family anymore. They would rather go far away from their family than feel awkward around them. Again, it is essential as parents to be verbal about your expectations from your living children and to help them understand their new roles in the "New Family."

Chapter 5

The Process of Grief

Grief may come in different forms and with different intensities, but it follows the same stages in everyone's life. Humans may differ in personal psychology, but we do share some similar behaviors. Some people think that the coping mechanisms they use are unique to them. We might have habits that we believe no one else has. However, we all share habits with other people, despite our unique personalities. This is one of the reasons why we can easily empathize with someone who is going through something critical in their life. At some point, we have been in their shoes.

Many incidents take place in our lives that rattle us to our very core. There is always going to be a breaking point where we shatter—it is necessary to get to that point to build ourselves back up again. We search for different ways to fix ourselves and our habits. Sometimes we succeed in fixing ourselves; other times we fail and have our spirits crushed. As sibling survivors, we always think that we have to rely on ourselves. We tell ourselves that our grief will never match the level of our parents' grief.

"Yes, I've lost a sibling. But they have lost a child. I can never reach their level of pain even if I tried thinking from their perspective."

We soothe ourselves with this idea because it helps us to avoid being confronted by our parents. We focus our thoughts on our parents to distract us from our own grief. It is an unhealthy coping mechanism because we don't know what we are supposed to feel at the moment. We feel as if our life has come to a complete halt, despite the world around us continuing at the same pace.

Suddenly, life becomes too much for us. Living becomes too much for us. At some point, we feel like

The Process of Grief

even breathing is too much of a hassle for us. With each breath we take, we feel our chest sinking in. We sleep and desperately wish for everything to be just one big nightmare.

However, with the next sunrise, we open our eyes and are faced with the same harsh reality. Do you know how it feels to have such vivid dreams where everything—right down to textures—feels real? And then suddenly, you open your eyes, and the person you wish to see the most is not there with you. Many sibling survivors out there try to sleep more because they prefer their fantasy over reality. There is not much one can do for us, and everything seems unreal. We question whether we are truly living, breathing creatures ourselves. We question our existence. Reality seems too blurry for us, and we believe that we are watching everything in our life being played out on a screen.

The sibling survivor feels like an outsider—someone who is merely watching something through a window. Grief detaches us from this world in a way that can be understood only if you go through it. We are too scared to ask our parents to hold us because we know that it will only make them fall apart. We destroy ourselves from the inside every day until we take the initiative to carry it out physically.

It never gets easy after you lose someone, especially a sibling. First, they leave this world physically and leave nothing but traces of their touches behind. Secondly, you lose their essence—we can't hold on to the departed sibling no matter what. We no longer can remember what they smelled like, what they felt like, how their smile slowly formed on their face.

Your arms refuse to remember how it felt to embrace them tightly. Thirdly, no amount of consoling will make us feel better. There comes a point where we isolate ourselves because the grief becomes too much to handle. At that moment, all we can do is try to touch their traces subtly. Lastly, your deceased child remains alive in just your memories, and that is what truly drives us insane with grief. Through time, we start to forget their voice, their expressions, and their habits.

All that remains is a fragment of memories that are at risk of being lost. We can lose our memories at any given moment. Memories can be altered to our liking, if we want. Our brains can alter these memories without any warning, and we are left behind wondering whether something really happened or not. Losing a child is like constantly living with physical and mental strain for the rest of your life. You can never truly overcome such strains and, hence, question the meaning of life.

Stages of Grief

To understand the grief of a sibling survivor, you need to understand the various stages of grief. Whether you want to believe it or not, grief is processed through five stages. Everyone goes through these phases when they come face-to-face with a loss. Whether it is abrupt or slow, losses hold the potential of making one live with guilt for eternity. Many sibling survivors wonder, *"Why did it have to be him or her? Why couldn't it have been me?"* One can truly understand such thinking processes if they understand what they are going through.

I don't like to say that grief is a problem. Many people deem grief problematic if it extends over a certain period. You don't understand that one can never, ever get over grief like this. Grief becomes a constant in the life of a sibling survivor, and to understand the reasons behind it, one must truly be educated on different stages of grief.

These stages of grief have been documented through countless amounts of research. The stages are shock, anger, denial, depression, and acceptance. I can openly talk about these stages because I, myself, have been through it. Losing my sister Lucy will forever be marked as the most traumatizing event of my life. There has been no greater loss, no greater pain, no greater emptiness in my life than the one left behind by the loss of my sister. Even thinking about her brings me pain when I remember that she is no longer a part of my life. A loss like that made me do things that, perhaps, I would not have done otherwise. It led me to make decisions I didn't think I would ever make like moving out of one state to another; which greatly upset my father.

By January of 1997, a month after Lucy's death, I had already gone through the first stage—shock—and was also working my way through the second and

The Process of Grief

third stages, anger and denial. Depression and anxiety had yet to show up when I was still trying to process the fact that my sister was gone. She was truly gone, and by "gone," I don't mean that she went away for a trip or finally moved out of my life.

I mean that she would never come back to me. She would never experience anything in this life, ever again. Her absence was too sudden, and it was obvious that it was bound to shock me. She died in a gruesome manner that got me stuck in a *"Why her?"* loop of questions. Worst of all was knowing that someone had stolen her life away from her. They stole her right to live and experience life; that is something that will always stick with me. My parents were stuck in that loop of questions and nightmares as well. That is the thing about grief: You can somehow fight your way through it, but it pains you to see loved ones going through similar hardships. This made me realize that both parents and living children stand in the same spot when they are going through these stages of grief. The pace one moves with when going through these stages might differ, but the thing is that you are all bound to go through it. Sometimes you may be at a stage behind your child, or a stage ahead, but, at the end of the day, you are going through it together.

What makes your living child's experience different from yours is the fact that they lack communication with you. They are sharing their grief with a close friend but might not be sharing it with you. I am sure you can see your child hurting, and you might even be able to guess what stage they are in to this very day. By understanding the stages of grief, you will be able to understand what your children are experiencing. This can also help you communicate with your grieving children a little better. I speak from my own experience, and I know that the majority can empathize with me.

Shock

Shock is probably one of the worst emotions present in humans. We like to think of depression as the worst, but shock is a numbing feeling that paralyzes all emotions. At this stage, you do not feel anything. There is a pause in your emotions, and that occurs when every emotion piles up until your brain freezes

The Process of Grief

up. After Lucy was killed, I remember how my mind had become numb. My mind was on autopilot, and I could not process through anything.

It was as if I was living but could not feel my own emotions. It was as if my mind and heart had become detached. The connection between these two was completely lost. My mind, my body, and my heart had crumbled under the pressure to the point where my thinking process was severed. I was sick, but, at the same time, I could not feel the symptoms. I could not diagnose myself with what it was because I just did not understand how I was hurting.

If anyone ever asked me what the worst stage of grief was, I would probably say that it was the "shock" stage. What came after that was just a rush of emotions that made me feel nauseous.

Anger
Yeah! I'm angry. Very angry. How could someone on the cusp of doing great things in her life be taken away? How could anyone steal her life away? How could anyone steal her away from *me*? The anger was so raw and powerful because I was finally feeling something

after being numb for a while. It was not fair how she got her life taken away from her without reason.

My mind was seething, and my eyes were seeing red. I did not know whether I was fine with the fact that I was finally feeling something or if I wanted to go back to the shock stage. At least when I was in the stage of shock, I did not have to confront all these feelings.

To get over my anger, I had to decide that, as unfair as it was, I would probably never understand why Lucy got killed. I wouldn't spin my wheels trying to figure it out. I could spend a lifetime trying to get answers and never succeed. I could have tried to talk to the killer and still not know why he killed her. I also would never have these answers, as he hung himself ten days after he killed Lucy. No amount of talking was going to make anything better either way. It was not going to change the fact that my sister was murdered and that she was gone for good. I was not eager to hear the killer's statement, either. He killed himself after taking my sister away from me, and, to this very day, this fact angers me. My thoughts would rear toward an ugly side that I wanted to suppress.

The Process of Grief

Maybe I did not want to hear any reason because nothing could justify her death. Lucy was gone for good, and no amount of searching for answers was ever going to bring her back to me. At this point, I was too angry to seek justice. I was stuck between wanting answers that were eating me up from the inside out, and making amends with the fact that Lucy would be gone even after I'd found the answers.

And alas, I chose peace over anger, which was harder than it sounds. Confronting the thought that even if I had the answers right in front of me, I did not have all the right questions in my head. I guess that's a Buddhist-like approach to being at peace with the decisions we make. Most of you might think that I was selfish to give up on it. However, it did calm me down from my anger. It made me stop blaming the world for all my problems. Nothing good in life ever comes if you start blaming the world for everything wrong that happens in your life. It was time to let go of the anger that was ruining my life. Choosing peace also helped me to stop blaming myself. My anger, no matter how justified, was not the answer to my loss. Hence, I moved on from anger and finally came face-to-face with denial.

Denial
Isn't it strange that despite knowing the truth, we sometimes still choose to deny it? We know it happened. We know they are gone but still can't admit it. There comes this halting thought that maybe everything that has happened up to this point has been nothing but a bad dream. I convinced myself that I was living in a nightmare. I would stay up at night and think, *"She's not dead."* She couldn't be dead because it just was not sinking in. Did I lose her? Lucy couldn't be dead because it just did not feel real.

I don't think this thought nearly as often as I did right after Lucy died, but I still feel it. I feel the denial deep inside of me as it pops up from time to time. I especially feel it around the beginning of December, when the anniversary of Lucy's death comes around. It feels as if someone has lodged something deep inside my throat, and I can neither swallow it nor spit it out. The feeling of denial is stuck deep inside my soul and makes it harder to breathe every year after her death anniversary. That is the day where I go through an entire whirlpool of emotions. On that day, I can feel myself going through all these five stages all at once.

It is hard for me to imagine that Lucy is gone to this very day. The thought is so incredibly complete. No matter how far I go in my life, I can still feel myself in denial of her death. It has been years but even if it were possible for a person to live for centuries, they would never get through this type of pain. This is rooted deep inside of you, and you can never get rid of it for the rest of your life.

Lucy is dead. What can I possibly do to change that? Nothing. Does that mean I jump into the acceptance stage? I wish.

Depression
Here we are, at one of the most frustrating stages of our lives, i.e., depression. This one ailment has ruined people's lives for as long as mankind has existed. It makes one lose a sense of self during this stage. The emotion of grief hits you so hard that it makes you take a step back. It seems as if there is no light in your life when you are drowning in depression. Depression

is like falling through a dark hole endlessly. Your head and heart both feel heavy. All you feel like doing is crying, but even that seems too much of a task for you. Surrendering yourself to depression should be avoided at all costs.

The first month after Lucy died, all I could do was drag myself out of bed and go to work. I remember being so incredibly tired. My body felt sluggish. It was like dragging my hand across a heavy current of water. I had to push myself to do a task as simple as taking a deep breath. I did not know why my body was physically slowing down. Why was I feeling tired even though I barely got out of bed on some days? I was getting plenty of sleep. I'd go to bed at nine o'clock at night and wake up the next day at eight.

I would get eight to ten hours of sleep every night and still wake up feeling unrested. On weekends, I would sleep longer than I had in ages. It was as if all I could do was sleep, sleep, and sleep my life away. I did not feel a sense of purpose in life. Not everyone faces depression in the same manner, though. The sibling survivors I have worked with either showed signs of insomnia or showed the same signs as I did. But at the end of the day, we would all feel restless and unsettled for the rest of our lives. Talking felt like too much of a burden, so I went quiet. I was so sapped of energy that it made me forget that I was alive, even if my sister Lucy no longer was.

After a few weeks, I was finally able to drag myself into the gym when the alarm went off in the morning, and I literally mean *drag*. I had decided that if I kept spending my time asleep, I, too, would expire mentally and physically. Going to the gym broke the chain of depression to an extent, because, by getting the exercise, I pumped up my body's endorphins and felt better. Exercising often helped me feel better. As I regained my energy, I regained my ability to initiate and carry on conversations.

In your grieving, I encourage you to make exercise a priority, too. You will appreciate what it does for you, both physically and mentally. I loosened up my tensed muscles (as depression can lead to locked muscles) and finally became capable of getting through it, even if I could never get "over" it.

Acceptance

Does anyone ever really accept that a brother or sister is gone forever? I don't know; that's a really big question here. I accept that an incredibly important chapter of my life—being a brother to Lucy—is over. I accept that I will no longer be able to talk to her and ask her opinions. I accept the fact that she will never get to meet the most important people in my life and vice versa. She will never meet my lovely wife or know my children—and they will never know her.

My daughters will never know about her, and she will never get to meet her own nieces. These thoughts make me sad every day as I try to push through life. I accept that I might never remember how her voice sounded. I accept everything, except for the fact that I have lost her forever.

But that doesn't mean that I don't know that she is dead. Of course, I do—I just refused to accept it for a very long period of my life. Accepting it would make everything so real, so I avoided that emotion altogether. Most sibling survivors avoid this stage as much as they can. They would rather stay stuck

The Process of Grief

in depression than ever come to terms with what is depressing them in the first place.

However, I also know that things happen and we don't understand why. There might not be an answer to everything in this life. There are going to be questions that will never be answered, no matter how hard we strive to achieve it. And I may never understand this while I live here on this mortal coil unless I accept it.

Finally, my acceptance helped me form a peace treaty with myself. When I knew that I can never know too much, then I was finally able to move on with my life. I can never move on from her death, but at least I can move on with my life to start a new chapter. It aches to think that she will forever be a part of my past—and never of my future. But maybe that is how things were supposed to be in the first place.

Sometimes surrendering to the truth of what we cannot control helps us gain control in return. Acceptance is coming to terms with your loss and your feelings. It makes you understand step by step what kind of thoughts you are going through. When you are finally done going through these stages of grief, you can clearly recall the times when you were stuck in a particular stage.

However, you need to make it through this to live on. Nothing good comes out of being stuck in a stage for the rest of your life. Accepting your loss—accepting the death of your sibling—can help you acquire a sense of peace. Acknowledging your grief comes after accepting the fact that your life from here on out is going to be tremendously different.

We, sibling survivors, have to accept the bitter reality to make it out alive through the grieving process. Even after the process of grief is completed, there are going to be days when one of these stages will pop back up in your life.

Chapter 6

Heal Yourself

I know how hard it is to heal yourself after going through traumatizing events in your life. Sometimes it sounds downright absurd when someone tells you that it is time to stop thinking about the past. Some say that thinking about the past is useless, but then again, those are the people who have not gone through what you have. Life is not a bed of roses. It is not always going to be rainbows and sunshine. But it is not always going to be hell, either. All of us go through a bad day, a bad week, or a bad month, and automatically assume that it is a bad life.

Why Don't They Cry?

It is not a bad life; it is merely a tough life. We are all going over one hurdle or another. But tackling the grief that comes with losing your sibling is the hardest situation. This is something you and I cannot "get over." None of us can get over something, your living children or someone who was such a prominent part of our life—those who were there with us from the beginning of time and those whom we thought would remain with us until the very end of it. That is one of the reasons why we can never truly get over any loss in life.

Siblings share the same life we do, and they can relate to us in ways no close friend can. Their ability to understand is far greater than you as parents' sometimes. Our siblings can understand us, help us, and move us in different ways. And suddenly one day, out of nowhere, we don't have that support system here with us anymore. They sometimes leave with "goodbye" and "I love you." Other times, it is abrupt, and they are suddenly no longer by our side. Siblings are a permanent part of our life, and to suddenly have that taken away from us can drive us insane.

They become a part of our memories instead of being a part of our life. We come to face the fact that they, too, were temporary, like so many other things in this life. They are no longer prominent. So, this makes us think, *"Can we get over something like this in our life?"* The answer is, "Of course not." Your living children can never let go of the pain and grief this loss brings them. But there is a point in our life where we need to end our suffering. By ending suffering, I am not talking about taking your own life. Healing is the first stage of ending your misery.

We think that our life is stuck, and somehow we cannot move forward. But we cannot step backward as well. We can never jump into our past to change things, but we can choose to step into our future to make it better. Life cannot simply end there, with your living children spending the rest of their life remaining depressed. Depression is an illness that kills you before you have the chance to die.

Do not let that emotion choke you until you can no longer breathe, eat, or sleep. There are many times I have fallen into severe depression whenever I think about my sister. The life we had and the memories we shared still cut deeply into my mind like a festering wound. But I pull myself out of it and tell myself that reminiscing and feeling pain is never going to help me.

I will forever look back and feel sadness, instead I should be looking back and feeling happy with the times I got to spend with Lucy. I always tell myself that these memories should be looked upon with nothing but positivity. Though it is hard not to feel sad about it sometimes, I still manage to find a way.

Of course, healing comes with a package of its own. It does not happen overnight, and we know that it is not going to happen in a year or two. Healing occurs at its own pace. It is an entirely different process for everyone who goes through it. Just like a wound that finally shuts closed, we need to let that pain go. There is no point in scraping at the wound until it becomes a hideous scar. The only thing we can do is let the wound heal, even if it is bone deep. Let it heal. I know that it is a long and tiring process. There were times when my parents were struck with grief so profound that it showed on their faces.

My mother admitted and shared one of her stories that will perhaps stick with me forever. She told me about the time when she put her hand into a coat pocket and found a receipt for a lunch she had with my sister a year before she died. It was very upsetting for her. She was honest with me about this, and she did tell me when it was hurting. Being honest about her reaction was certainly very important to me. Yes, as a parent, you have to take care of your grief and also, make sure that your living child is not spiraling into depression. Being honest and talking it out is one of the best ways to let your living child know that they are not alone in this pain.

They get a sense of understanding, and perhaps they will let their defenses crumble. If you are having a bad day, or something is tough for you, and you are talking to your child, don't tell them that everything is okay. Your living child thinks that nothing is ever going to be bad in their life. Living children, especially those who are in their pre-pubescent years, believe that their life is going to be the same. Teenagers think differently from adults. And, as a parent, you must know that very well. We have all gone through a rebellious stage as teenagers—we don't know how to act.

We are treated like a child yet expected to make decisions like adults. It is a confusing stage for everyone, but it passes by. Be real and honest with your living children. Talk to them like you would with your colleague or a close friend. Do not be afraid to stand up and say, *"I am having a tough day."* They may not share their feelings, but at least, I can almost guarantee that, as an adult child, I appreciate it when my parents let me know what they are going through. Humans have a strange nature of helping others, even though they too are going through a tough time. We all like to go out of our way to help those who share experiences similar to ours.

But the thing is that you can never really help anyone else unless you heal yourself before deciding to help others. You can never truly help anyone, and no one will seek your help when they see how wounded you are. To appear more reliable, you must love yourself enough to take care of yourself. Of course, it is never going to be easy. We always hesitate when it comes to helping ourselves. We tell ourselves that it is a complete hassle, and, at times, we even think that it's not worth it. It gets even harder when you become a parent.

As we grow up, we finally understand what our parents were going through while raising us. Parents are the only people who are willing to make endless sacrifices for you and for the sake of your happiness. They kill off their own wants, needs, and desires to focus on their children solely. As a child, you might never truly understand the sacrifices made by your parents until you find yourself walking in their shoes. All I can tell the parents at this point is to make sure that they take care of themselves the way they take care of their own children.

As a parent myself, I know how easy it becomes to lose your own identity as you venture down the road of parenthood. Everything stops being about "me," and it starts being about "my kid." When your child is going through the flu, you run back and forth from hospitals to make sure that it goes away. But when we, the parents, come down with the flu, we brush it off as something that will pass. You know that you have to get over being sick before you can take care of them. But this loss, the loss of your child, is not something you can shrug off like you did when you felt sick.

Why Don't They Cry?

You cannot simply tell yourself to focus solely on your child. If you are not doing well and are not in a good space yourself, it is much harder for you to help your children. I know how hard it is for you to see your child suffering, but you simply cannot overlook your own suffering. To help your child heal, you (the parents) need to heal first. We all have our separate journeys, and you need to realize that your children will have a journey that is completely different from your own. All of us have to walk down this path of life and travel down this road of loss, but we end up dealing with it in different ways. The loss you are experiencing is one of two different types of losses. You have lost a child who died, but your living child has lost a sibling, too. It is harder to step into each other's shoes to see their point of view. But just because it is difficult doesn't mean that it is entirely impossible. Again, the importance of simply talking to your child is much more crucial than we care to think about.

As a parent, you need to find your way down this road somewhat before you can start to help your children. It is important to let your kids know that you are here for them. You can still talk to them even if they are not ready to take you up on it. Honesty is quite difficult to accomplish as an adult. Admitting things out loud suddenly makes everything real for you, and you refuse to let it out. As a parent, you need to take counseling or other means to heal before you can help your child with it.

Conveying your feelings may seem scary to you. You feel the need to tiptoe around your children, but the problems do not simply vanish if you refuse to talk about it. By being open and honest yourself, you are passing on the wisdom of honesty down to your living child. You are telling them, *"I know it's hurting, but it's okay to let people know when you do. Bottling it up is only going to make your grief stay with you forever. Stop hurting yourself, and tell me what's bothering you. I'll be honest with you, and I'll patiently wait for you to be honest with me."*

It gives you a mild sense of relief to know that you have at least communicated. You need to tell them that you are here for them before letting them come to you for comfort. In this way, each of you can help the other during your tough days. It may also be helpful for your children to have some sort of counseling or therapy along the way. There are many grief coaches in this world who specifically focus on helping families and individuals work through their grief.

It sometimes sounds like a joke to many families going through this loss, but most of them end up taking on the grief coaches to help themselves. Hiring a mental health counselor is also a great way to work through some of the issues. It is important for everybody to have someone outside of the family to talk to. Talking to those who can give you an overview of your life and your grief from a different perspective can be effective sometimes. They can help you understand things you cannot understand on your own. This is one of the many reasons why I urge most sibling survivors to talk about their pain to someone outside the family. Letting out your emotions can help you start with the healing process. This is one of the reasons you should always have someone by your side to help you get through this pain. Grief is not something you have to go through alone, and, in fact, you probably shouldn't. You should find someone, like a friend who promises to

Heal Yourself

be there for you, or a professional who is qualified to help you. This can help you understand your pain and psychology better before you can start healing yourself. Tell your children to find someone who they can talk to as well.

Sometimes, family therapy can help with old wounds. When a family comes together, it is best to let out all your complaints so that you can go back to your life with fewer burdens. When we leave things unspoken, we are allowing our thoughts to weigh down on us horribly. It is better to heal those wounds and help the family collectively move past this horrible, horrible chapter in your life. Another thing that has been helpful for many other sibling survivors, including myself, is a creative project to express the feelings that they are having.

I happened to make a video of all of the places my sister and I grew up in, the schools that she went to, and some of the places that we went together. This was very cathartic for me. Others may write poetry, paint, or make sculptures. Some may volunteer at an organization that your deceased child was particularly fond of as a way of giving back and honoring them. This also may be helpful for you as a parent. If you do something together, it is a way for all of you to share something—beyond just being there and talking about how each other is feeling and how you are doing.

These are good questions to ask, but you may not get the answers. However, if you are collectively doing a creative project together, it may open up the channels of communication for you. There are many organizations available to help you through this loss. Compassionate Friends is one of the great organizations filled with other parents who have lost a child. Surrounding yourself with others who have been in a similar situation is sometimes very comforting.

They can understand what you feel, as they have been down this road. You may find that this organization or a similar one can be helpful in healing yourself, and it is equally important that your living children heal themselves and find their way through this loss. It is one of the best forms of therapy for you and your child. This is highly recommended to those going through such grief because, at some point, this grief takes a turning point and develops into madness.

We need to get ourselves out of that madness ourselves. There was a parent who came to me seeking help, and seeing her transition truly inspired me to believe that therapy can do wonders for a person. Judith is the mother of four who lost her youngest daughter about five years ago. She was utterly devastated at the loss of her daughter, as is any parent. She was not quite sure what to do, either. It was obvious that losing her child made her lose direction in life.

One day, she expressed the feeling of being lost and unstable from time to time. She did not feel like she was able to be a good mom, a good wife, or a good friend to anyone anymore. Her loss had shaken her to her core, and she was questioning whether going through this was worth the pain. She was so overwhelmed by her grief, that she knew that she could no longer stall her own life. She needed to get back on her feet for the sake of her family, yet she barely felt the energy to do it. Judith did not know where to turn for help. She was reluctant when it came to mental therapy, as she'd been raised in a time when mental health therapy was not given any serious importance. This generation focuses more on mental health, and it made her seek mental health therapy to see what it was. She was always taught to believe that mental health therapy was for those who were mad. That was for people who were *"crazy,"* and she was not crazy.

Judith did admit that there were days when she felt that she might be losing her mind. She was so overwhelmed by her grief that, in her mind, she truly thought she was going crazy. Later, through endless searching, she happened to stumble upon the Compassionate Friends Group. She attended one of the meetings held by the group. She found it helpful, although she knew that she needed more help. Finally, Judith decided to seek more help for her sake. Going to therapy truly helped change her life. It gave her the tools and the words that she needed to hear to be able to start processing her grief.

Not only that, but Judith found it very healing to go and volunteer in a middle school where she helped kids with math and science. Judith had been very good at math and science in college. She'd helped her kids from time to time with these subjects and decided to help others. She told me that she found a lot of satisfaction in being able to help other children who were about the same age as her youngest daughter. This made her feel motherly toward this particular age group, and she expressed how it helped her. My interest in her process was growing, and I finally asked Judith whether she would continue in the middle school or transition to high school.

Her response made me think how intriguing it is to see someone change so drastically. She said she liked the middle schools and that the kids were very challenging at that age, full of a lot of attitude—and that she liked it. The children reminded Judith of her daughter when they sassed back at her. It helped her stay in the moment. As you can see, Judith chose the path to healing herself, and, through that healing, she did for herself, she was able to help her family and other people. She reports that although she misses her daughter every day, she finds that her grief does not have that overwhelming effect because she was able to do some healing for herself.

It made me realize that people in our life come for a reason and that they leave for a reason. They change us by simply being there for us, and they hold the power to change even after they have left us. I never thought I would be helping other sibling survivors, but here I am. I have come this far and helped others who are going through the same grief because it helped me heal myself.

I hope that, through this book, you find the courage to move on with life without holding any regrets. Find ways that can heal you in a way that will no longer hurt you. Find ways to connect with your living children because they are still there for you, and they still need you, no matter what they say. It is natural for you, as parents, to help your children. But it is somehow natural for children to help you as well. This is the only relationship that works both ways in life.

It is not easy to heal and forget, but it will get easier to bear this pain after you finally heal yourself.

Chapter 7

How Are Your Parents?

Humans, by nature, lose their true identities when they fall into a pit of grief. We all see a change in people when they lose their temper, so it is natural for them to lose a part of themselves during their grief process. The process is long and tiring, but at the end of the day, you still need to overcome it. Sorrow is an ugly emotion that can make someone lose their sense of self. Hence, it is a common occurrence that parents lose a part of their identity after the loss of a child.

You may understand this grieving process by imagining how much time, attention, and strength it takes to get a child into this world and raise them.

Why Don't They Cry?

A child is everything for a parent. People may do whatever they want when they are independent and do not have anyone else dependent upon them. But real change for a human begins when they step into the world of parenthood. It is just normal human psychology to be more responsible when you have someone depending on you for guidance and support.

Parents are protective by nature, but there are still some parents who often lose themselves during their process of grief. Sadly, having that part of their parenthood snatched away from them can forever leave them in the heartbroken stage. As I said earlier, for a parent, their child is everything. There is an entire process involved in bringing a child into this world. It does not happen as they show in the movies. The woman does not randomly become pregnant and they fast-forward to the delivery day, as if the nine months in between were nonexistent.

Our *real* lives are quite different from the movies. The movies have a knack of making everything easy, and that is why most people enjoy watching movies

How Are Your Parents?

in the first place. But as any parent would know, life is not like a movie. The entire birthing process is not as chaotic as they sometimes show it to be in movies to increase the drama, but it is not easy, either. You could say that everything starts within those nine months, and you are led to believe that it will last a lifetime. Parents take great pains to bring a part of themselves and their partner into this world through the miraculous process of birthing.

I believe that each parent shares their bond with their child differently. A mother shares the longest relationship with her child, despite the presence of the father, due to the nine months of pregnancy. A father gets to experience everything about their unborn baby through the mother of their child. He may observe the movements of the child inside the womb of his significant other, but he is not in the actual shoes of the mother. A mother is left sick for months, and the after-effects of the birth last for up to two or three years. A child, for her, is her absolute everything—a part of her.

Be it her first child, or her second or third, she still shares a connection with the baby when it is nothing but a bunch of cells residing in her womb. Therefore, it is universally acknowledged that the mother shares a connection that may transcend even a miracle. Of course, it differs for everyone out there. Just because the mother is in direct contact with the fetus doesn't mean that she is the only one who has a strong connection with the unborn child. The father holds many hopes and desires in his heart as he counts down the arrival of the baby every day, too. He is always there by the mother's side, soothing and calming her down during her rainy days. He is the support system the mother needs because he knows that she is the carrier and, therefore, the most important person in his life.

Of course, you may perceive this to be some sort of a fairytale or movie-like example, but those who are committed to this know how important these eight to nine months are. As a father myself, I have observed how the whole "becoming a father" does not feel real until you hold the baby in your arms. We, as humans, crave physical evidence so that we, too, can share an emotional connection with the baby the same way a mother does.

How Are Your Parents?

I still remember the first time I held my firstborn daughter in my arms. Holding that tiny, precious baby close to my heart for the very first time filled me with pride. I may have not done much in life, but knowing that I'd had a part in creating something as beautiful as this new creature, full of life, filled me with pride. Honestly, it scared me to realize that I would go to the ends of the Earth just to bring joy to her. She was so tiny and so exquisite to hold. She had the power to move me with just a simple, soft cry. Becoming a parent finally made me realize that, as soon as you become one and enter the journey of parenthood, your life will suddenly start revolving around that child. Some parents get drunk off their happiness as they become parents. No matter how tiring the entire process of becoming a parent is, in the end, it is all worth it. Every sacrifice you make becomes worth more than millions of dollars when you hold your child. The entire world stops for you as you fall into the ritual of catering to every need of your newborn child.

Becoming a parent myself made me finally understand my parents' loss. What they went through is something I would not wish upon my worst enemy.

This realization dawned on me only when I went out of my way to imagine myself in their shoes. That obviously did not sit well with me, and it shattered me to know that I was not even capable of putting myself in their shoes, while they had to experience all of it.

Losing that connection with your child can push you into a sudden, major state of shock. It is completely understandable when they suffer through the shock, as losing a child is a traumatizing process. But you somehow pull yourself out of it for the sake of your children. And by that, I mean *some* parents are able to overcome their grief with the passage of time. There are a few parents who refuse to come out of their shocked state despite the amount of therapy they receive. They completely lose focus of themselves and forget to focus on their living children. Like many things in this world, there are two extremes to choose from as a way of reacting to a major trauma such as losing a child.

Either the parents would be too protective of their living child or they would completely neglect the grieving child by focusing on themselves. Parents are humans, too, but they hold responsibility for more than just themselves. Their pain is justified, but their negligence can never be.

Effects of Negligence

More often than not, some siblings who talk about parents who do not focus on their surviving offspring. These children feel left out or entirely forgotten, and rightfully so. I am not saying that a parent should not focus on their own grief; they have the right to do that. What I'm trying to say is that they do not have to focus on their grief all alone. You need to realize that parents share the same connection as you do with your sibling—but it's ten times stronger than yours.

"Negligence" may be a harsher term to use here regarding the pain of a survivor sibling. After all, negligence is all about maltreatment of children that is not age appropriate. It is a form of child abuse that can have serious repercussions in other contexts. In severe cases, the parent might end up losing all custodial rights to their own child. Crazy, right?

Think of ignoring your living child's pain as a form of negligence from your perspective.

It is not enough that you provide them with shelter and get them to a therapist. Expecting them to get better through mental health therapy is a good option, but that should not be the only option. Ignoring the needs of your living child is a common occurrence that I have observed in families approaching me with a cry for help.

The parents completely revert to focusing on themselves. Some do this with the best of intentions. The parents believe that fighting their grief and overcoming it can only help them when they reach the point of helping their child. But that is not the case, parents need to be aware of the fact that pain caused by losing a child can never truly go away. Losing a child is like losing a part of yourself—forever gone, out of your reach. It makes them believe that it is the end of their world and that they will never be able to get their life back together. So, they rely on medicating and soothing themselves for the rest of their lives, while never reaching the point of helping their child overcome it. It is natural to be a shield for your child, but it also seems natural to you to indulge yourself in that one loss of yours. This can make you lose sight of people you have yet to lose. When most sibling survivors talk to me, they tell me how they feel left out of the lives of their parents.

"It's as if they have completely forgotten about me. Do I not matter as much to them now?" Even if we think that "negligence" is too harsh a word to use in this case, unfortunately, that is the case in the child's world. Most surviving siblings would even say how they feel "neglected." The concept of negligence actually goes beyond the physical pain of being away from their parents. It is a form of emotional abuse that the parents unknowingly and subconsciously inflict on their children.

High Divorce Rates

A lot of married couples end up splitting after the loss of a child. Be it the loss of their only child, or a loss of one of several children, they end up in a situation that makes them feel as if the loss of their child has made them lose a sense of love between them. They end up believing that their lost child was the only thing holding them together. They lose a sense of direction and end up splitting without thinking about the damage it would do to their surviving child. This is only because the couple is unable to cope with the death of their child and comes to believe that splitting is the only thing that can help them overcome their pain.

Most people start with comments such as, *"It's amazing how your marriage has survived such a loss."* That reflects the severe impact, child loss has had on the marriage. Outsiders will say how lucky you are to still have other kids and not realize how insensitive their remarks are. After dealing with such comments, the parents decide that they can no longer live together while grieving for someone who had brought such great joy into their life. This loss may put a heavy strain on your marriage, and seeing your parents get divorced during such a vulnerable moment is probably the last thing your children want to witness. It can greatly harm the living child in more ways than just one. Seeing such a strain between the parents makes the living child question their worth and makes them wonder what the purpose of their life is to begin with. This can even lead them toward suicidal tendencies, and that is something the grieving couple should be cognizant of.

Divorce itself can bring out a plethora of trust issues in children and might jade them even further. Parents need to keep in mind that their living child has as much say in this as them. After all, at the end of the day, they are left with "taking a side"—which parent they want to live with—and that can result in another traumatizing experiences.

During this time, the parents are mostly focusing on themselves. They are putting their own wants and needs before the children's. This is understandable; there is so much emotional baggage and grief to deal with. But the act of divorce is more than just a selfish act on the part of the bereaved parents. This is their way of coping with their loss, and the only option they feel left for them is accepting the change because they can never go back to the way it was. It almost seems like all the love and the spark is gone between the parents. Looking into another grieving face that resembles your own can drive you crazy. You do not want to be alone, but at the same time, you do not want to share the pain with someone else, either. The parents lose a sense of togetherness because adapting to change is much easier than accepting the loss of something. Hence, a divorce takes place. The loss of a child may be the straw that breaks the back of an already-strained, on-the-verge-of-breaking-up relationship. But for a child, it is another distressing experience for them to go through. Losing a sibling and facing the separation or divorce of your parents—all at the same time? That could make them come completely undone.

They will start forgetting what is real and what is fake. This will burden your child with a bunch of trust issues that can later harm their future. That is, if your living child decides to have a future after witnessing such tragedies all in one go. There is a reason for couples counseling. There are certainly times when every couple is challenged in their marriage. The loss of a child is one of the biggest challenges. I have seen couples in which one partner is just not able to accept the loss and is having a hard time moving forward to process their grief. It can be hard to work as a team if you are not both in a similar place. There are, of course, many reasons that couples undergo a divorce, but I would like to just implore that you consider the effect it will have on your living children. Breaking up during such a difficult part of your life will bring temporary relief but permanent regrets. You cannot undo whatever choice you make, so thinking about your living child should always be on the top of your priorities list when it comes to breaking your family apart.

"I'm fine."
Let me tell you something: The living children may say that they are fine, but they are, in fact, far from being fine. You need to realize that the only reason the living children say this is that they believe that you need your space. You might be the most caring person in this world, but you may have accidentally made your living children feel worthless. It is normal to grieve over a loss, but to be stuck with it is something that is not normal. They fake their well-being for your sake, and at the end of the day, you do not even acknowledge their response. Your

living child is not fine, even when they say or show you that they are.

The reason behind the hard exterior of the living child is that they are not sure themselves how they are feeling half of the time. They do not know whether life is truly worth living because they have lost one of their biggest supporters. You are the adult here, the one with wisdom, so do not expect them to know better. Be there to guide them.

Forgotten Mourners

Sibling Survivors are often termed "forgotten mourners" because they portray a tough image of themselves. I cannot stress enough the importance of how sibling survivors are always forgotten. Their mourning is always overlooked, and they are forever left in the back seat of the grief wagon, whereas the parents take the front wheel.

Siblings can survive while being ignored by the world, but they can never survive being ignored by their own parents, especially when it comes to acknowledging grief. Some parents focus on themselves rather than on their child. When they do focus on their living child, they often do it in a negative way.

"If only your brother/sister were here. They would do this, they would do that." Four out of every ten sibling survivors have dealt with this kind of negative attention every once in a while. You might think that this is the best way to help them understand their new responsibility and their new role in the family, but it only helps to make your living children resentful of their deceased siblings.

Do not compare your living children with the ones you have lost. This will only create unwanted tension in your household and can cause them to become distant from you. Every sibling survivor will start questioning your love for them. It is a natural response, as every human is born with this defense mechanism. How would you like it if your children started differentiating between the parents? Every parent plays a different role, and expecting them to do something that does not fit into their role is strange—right?

Then why do you fail to realize that every child in your life is born to play a different role? The sibling order determines what role each child will play. The eldest will be the most responsible one, so you train them from a very young age to take care of their younger siblings. The youngest will be the most spoiled one, so you let your youngest child get away with a lot of things. The middle child plays the role of a mood-maker and a peacemaker who holds up the balance between the eldest and the youngest one. They fall into these roles naturally, and asking them to step out of their given role just because one of them leaves is like asking them to give up their identity. You have your own identity and are playing a certain role when you enter parenthood.

Having that chunk of identity going to waste is unbearable, but you have to let it go. Your deceased child, no matter how precious, is no longer there to receive your love. You can love them only from beyond the grave. However, just because you have lost one child or two does not mean that you stop focusing on your living child. They are still there with you and are still waiting for you to come out of your grieving stage just so you can hold them.

How Are Your Parents?

Being a parent or a child is tough, but we must all move past the damage to build something better for the living child. Going back to the life you had before your loss is impossible, but moving through that loss to build something new is still an option. You will never get over losing your child, and your living children will never get over the loss of their sibling, but you all can continue to work your way through the loss. Remember that you can define your loss and not the other way around. Do not let your loss hold this power over you. It does not need to define you.

Hanging on to losses without realizing what you have will forever haunt you if you do not realize the worth of your living children at the right moment. No one can replace a parent for a child, and no child can become a replacement for the child you have lost. Accepting that bitter pill will be painful at first, but it is the reality of your life now, and you need to accept it to move through it.

About the Author

Zander Sprague is a two-time sibling survivor international best-selling author, and Professional Clinical Counselor for Sibling Loss. He holds a Master's degree in Mental Health Counseling and works to raise the awareness of Sibling Survivors.

Part of this important work is with parents to help them understand their living child's grief. He lives in the San Francisco Bay Area and is a father and an avid road cyclist.

CPSIA information can be obtained
at www.ICGtesting.com
Printed in the USA
JSHW031242310123
37107JS00003B/160